Robert Bly

2000 *Distinguished Artist*

THE McKNIGHT FOUNDATION

The Art of Poetry

Between shadows and clearing, between defenses and young girls,
having inherited an original heart, and funereal imagination,
suddenly pale, something withered in my face,
in mourning like a desperate widower every day of my life,
for every drop of invisible water I drink
in my sleepy way, and for every sound I take in shivering,
I have the same chilly fever, and the same absent thirst,
an ear coming into the world, an oblique anxiety,
as though robbers were about to arrive, or ghosts,
inside a seashell with great and unchangeable depths,
like a humiliated waiter, or a bell slightly hoarse,
like an aged mirror or the smell of an empty house
where the guests come in hopelessly drunk at night,
having an odor of clothes thrown on the floor, and no flowers,
—in another sense, possibly not as sad—
still, the truth is, the wind suddenly hitting my chest,
the nights with infinite substance fallen into my bedroom,
the crackling of a day hardly able to burn,
ask from me sadly whatever I have that is prophetic,
and there are objects that knock, and are never answered,
and something always moving, and a name that does not come clear.

Pablo Neruda (translation, Robert Bly)

Introduction

Many writers in this book can claim friendship with Robert Bly, can testify personally to the uniqueness and magnitude of his literary contributions. I'm not one of them. I'm one of the tens of thousands of readers and admirers who have known him only through the printed page, through his poems.

The important body of literary work he's produced over five decades is reason enough to single out and celebrate him, but it is Bly the relentless teacher who amazes me. The more I read about how many people—from neighbors to renowned poets—he has helped, taught, nudged, stretched, entertained, and enlightened, the greater my admiration grows.

His work never shrinks from the truth, from making judgments, from explaining things differently—even when it's unpopular. But that penetrating honesty is matched by a generosity of spirit that has touched scores of lives—from the days when his Madison farmhouse was a mecca for young Midwest poets to the courses he offered residents of his hometown and his memorable readings and performances worldwide.

Perhaps the most obvious proofs of his generosity are the Scandinavian, South American, European, Indian, and Middle Eastern poets whose work he translated into English, often introducing them for the first time to readers in the United States. He could hardly have given us a finer gift than those richly hued, passionate new voices.

Although the branches of his influence and work reach far beyond our state borders, Robert Bly—like the previous two distinguished artists—has deep roots here. I am delighted that we honor him now specifically as a Minnesota poet. By staying here all these years, he has certainly honored us.

Noa Staryk
Chair
The McKnight Foundation

Contents

Midwestern Sublime

By Patricia Hampl

obert Bly's celebrity as the author of the provocative prose work *Iron John* has in some ways obscured his extraordinary lifetime accomplishment as a poet and translator, as an editor of great influence, and as a champion of the best literary values of the age.

Beginning with his earliest work—the transparent poems of *Silence in the Snowy Fields* and *The Light Around the Body*—Robert Bly annunciated a fresh American voice that (along with the work of his friend James Wright which he edited and published) liberated the American poetic enterprise from academic strictures at a time when poetry and literature in general were held captive to a brittle and arch sensibility.

I am sketching this landscape with broad strokes, but I must speak of this moment in literary history—the mid-'60s—from personal memory. I was an English undergraduate at the University of Minnesota then, and experienced the dramatic change of the period at firsthand. There were no creative writing classes in the English Department, and there was no Loft, no "literary community" in the Twin Cities. We were encouraged, as English majors, to study British, not American, writers, and especially writers of the past. Nothing wrong with that—except for the exclusivity that came with this injunction. The Metaphysical poets of the seventeenth century were always preferred to Whitman, for example, who was considered at best an eccentric, at worst a barbarian. Indeed, James Wright, whom we recognize now as one of the enduring voices of the age, was denied tenure at the university, and left for New York. Needless to say, there were no courses on women's literature or African American writers. Allen Tate, the poet in residence in the department, reigned frostily, working mostly with graduate students who fervently aspired to his exquisite hauteur. It was the age that made of T. S. Eliot, another Midwesterner, a cultural icon of priestly stature. But of course, Eliot had turned himself into an English poet, and it was for this magic act, in great measure, that he was held in such reverence by Tate and the masters of the moment.

Robert Bly was living in western Minnesota with his young family on his family's farm at this time, writing the beautiful, unencumbered poems of *Silence in the Snowy Fields* which opened my eyes and ears to the lyric possibilities of the contemporary American vernacular—and an unapologetic Midwestern vernacular at that—the very voice I had been taught to disdain in my classes. He was also editing his influential magazine *The Fifties* (by then *The Sixties,* and still later *The Seventies*—a magazine that must have driven the cataloguers at the Library of Congress mad).

I first heard of Robert Bly when I bought a copy of his magazine and discovered there an immediacy and pulse in poetry I had not found in my classes. Here were the poems, translated by Bly, of Pablo Neruda and Vallejo and Lorca, poems also from Sweden and Norway—a wide world of poetry rushing into my life, spilling over the narrow confines of the *Norton Anthology of English Literature*. I read Bly's magazine, and his good-spirited but deadly attacks on the literary establishment, and I knew I was reading the future.

That was the first conversion. There were two to follow. When I read *Silence in the Snowy Fields,* I experienced one of those galvanizing moments that change everything. I simply understood (and this is not convenient hindsight: I saw it at the time) that everything that had been dismissed about the world around me and which, unwittingly, I was being educated to dismiss was in fact the material of a life's work, the reason to be a poet at all. We—this place and this life—had not been *told.* The voice of our life right-here-right-now had not been rendered, and Robert Bly (and James Wright, whom I discovered at the same time) was refusing to turn himself into a faux English poet in order to win the prizes that came with that bargain. What I loved and still love and am forever grateful for in Bly's work is that he uncovered the lyric voice for us all—our own lyric voice, not a borrowed one. Read the poems of *Silence* today and the freshness of the idiom is still invigorating, still enlarging.

The first poetry reading I attended (this was an era of few readings, always culturally reverent, stuffy events) was one Bly organized and at which he read. It was an antiwar reading, and here Robert Bly provided a third eye-opener. It is difficult to re-create the extraordinary polarization of the Vietnam War years. It was not at all clear at the time whether Bly and the other poets who participated in these antiwar readings would be arrested and jailed. They were actively encouraging draft-age young men to refuse to serve; they were writing and reading poetry that was telling the political truth against their own government. It was scary, and it was courageous. And it made poetry absolutely essential, and as real as the bread and roses we sang about.

I dwell on this early period because it is important to see Robert Bly's contribution in historic terms—he is a figure that large, that consequential. He cannot simply be praised for the quality of his work. He is a protean writer, with an astonishing output. His contributions to translation in America, alone, deserve an award. His own poetry remains, to this day with the latest work, evergreen and a model of what could be called the Midwestern sublime. He has of course been profoundly influenced by the surrealism of Latin American poets, but he is not a mere imitator.

I must also mention Robert Bly's unprecedented generosity towards other, especially younger and unknown, writers. I count myself as a recipient of his kindness, and I know of many others. In the '60s and '70s there were no MFA programs or "workshops" in the area. It became known—I can't remember how—that if you sent a batch of your poems to Robert Bly, he would reply. And he did—thoughtfully, promptly, generously—and with a fiercely honorable candor that alone can extend true respect to a beginning writer. A response like that can keep a young writer going. There are many of us who will never forget that generosity and the bracing experience of editorial honesty. It may be what's best about the literary life here. That spirit certainly began with Robert Bly.

Robert Bly has written books people detest and argue over—with reason. He is not simply another beloved Minnesota writer, harmless and endearing. He is a figure we will puzzle over always, as indeed American poetry will. It is precisely for his paradoxical mixture of grandeur and simplicity that I treasure him. I cannot imagine my own reading and writing life without his work and his buoyant example. More to the point, I can't imagine American literature without him.

Patricia Hampl is an author and a Regents' Professor and McKnight Distinguished Professor in the Creative Writing Program of the Department of English, University of Minnesota. She lives in the Twin Cities.

Back to the Snowy Fields

By Wayne Dodd

G o back now twenty years later and you will still find it, lying silently in ditches beside the road, drifting noiselessly in with the snow at nightfall, standing dry and bristly in a field of weeds: *The spirit of the American prairie*. For that is what Robert Bly discovered for us in *Silence in the Snowy Fields:* the spirit of the American (prairie) landscape. Nowhere a trace, not one blurring linger, of language or perception from another culture or geography (all influences of Spanish, Chinese, Latin American—and other—poets notwithstanding). Just the American land, breathing into and through Bly. And us. I would even go so far as to say, if pressed, that however much else Bly may have contributed to the ferment of American letters, this has been perhaps his most important contribution—aside from the rich offering of the poems themselves. Once we had experienced *Silence in the Snowy Fields,* the body of America was never again the same to us—never again "merely" there, never again *external* to our own locus of spirit, no longer obedient to even the most carefully translated commands from "English" poetry. Since *Silence,* a developing generation of new young poets has been able to take for granted the subtle and important knowledge of our geographical lives that these poems provide. It has come to be a given, something which, once gained, one can never go back from: like self-consciousness. It has become a fundamental fact of, not just a *way* of knowing, but also a *what*.

But perhaps *consciousness* would be the more useful term, because it is consciousness that these poems are concerned with, consciousness of the world of solitude, of darkness, of isolation, of silence. That's what these poems are in touch with—the other world: sleep, the hidden, the unseen; what might be called *the rest of it*. That's what the silence is filled with, what it frees us for: the other half, the realm of dark knowledge, night. . . .

Poem after poem in this remarkable book successfully enlarges a bare-bones narrative, exemplum-like in its simplicity, with an incomparably greater sense of existence, a complex presence of life. We come to be aware, as Bly is aware, of the abiding presence of a hidden order, the sacred masked by the ordinary. Poems arrive to suddenly opened vistas:

> We know the road; as the moonlight
> Lifts everything, so in a night like this
> The road goes on ahead, it is all clear.
> ("After Working")

or to vague, indefinable threats:

> The barn is full of corn, and moving toward us now,
> Like a hulk blown toward us in a storm at sea;
> All the sailors on deck have been blind for many years.
> ("Snowfall in the Afternoon")

There is a sense of *duende* about the darkness, "like a paling sky reminding [us] of death." So much happens in these poems at the very moment of shift—from day to night, from sleeping to waking, etc. Events suddenly open up like doors, and a world walks strangely and disturbingly in. . . .

And always we are aware of our bodies—stiff-fingered and clumsy with cold, or alive like a harbor at dawn, or alert to the sound of corn stalks in the wind, to the dark pull of a spot of earth we could feel safe in, to the odor of leaves on the wet earth, to the feel of moonlight on our branches. And then we are, at last, fully inside the land of ourselves. "If I reached my hands down, near the earth," we say,

> I could take handfuls of darkness!
> A darkness was always there, which we never noted.

So after *Silence in the Snowy Fields* we were never quite the same again, either. The darkness in us was never the same again. Nor the snow that covers the bare fields waiting always behind our eyes. Nor the barns we hold ourselves to the remembered earth by. Nor the houses we are adrift in—in Minnesota, Ohio, Michigan, Illinois, and elsewhere all over the great body of the land our breath freezes and warms in. Sometimes, now, a cowbell sounds from so deep within us, or the eyes of a horse gaze so clearly into our consciousness, that we wake suddenly into the present which *Silence in the Snowy Fields* seems always to have been a bright—and dark—part of.

Wayne Dodd is a writer and the editor of The Ohio Review. *He lives in Athens, Ohio. This excerpt is from an essay that originally appeared in* When Sleepers Awake *(ed. Joyce Pesseroff, University of Michigan Press, Ann Arbor, 1984). Reprinted by permission of the author.*

Bly's Later Poems

By Charles Molesworth

Bly is still, and probably always will be, an extremist, a poet willing to put his talent not only to the test, but to the task of a demanding vision. For him, poetry can never be a "border of ideas," as it was for Pound's Lady Valentine, nor is it a criticism of life in any safe, humanistic way. Bly's poetry is fundamentally a challenge, and what has been clarified in the last fifteen years is the set of terms in which he issues that challenge.

The publication of *This Body Is Made of Camphor and Gopherwood* (1977) signals a decisive change in Bly's poetry. Though continuing to use the prose-poem, as he had in *The Morning Glory* (1975), Bly concentrates his vision more directly on ecstatic moments, and writes what must be described as religious poetry. . . .

What is distinctive about *Camphor and Gopherwood* is the persistence and dominance in it of the religious impulse. Or, to put it in broader terms, Bly exemplifies the curious persistence of theological modes of experience and feeling in our present-day, secularized culture. This persistence often poses a scandal for criticism. For many readers, especially those with secularized imaginations, Bly's work strikes a thoroughly false and, what is worse, an utterly outmoded note. For others, the religious is simply assimilated to that other category, the supercharged "poetic," a post-Arnoldian preserve of the literary, where we safely store away all that is not marketable, all that is not "operative" in today's society. These readers are likely to overpraise Bly, to read him with little critical or historical awareness, and to accept his religious yearnings simply as a sort of Jungian compensation and corrective to technocratic thought. It is difficult to know a way other than these two alternatives, the dismissive and the obsequious. The former often degenerates into *ad hominem* attacks, while the latter becomes a twisted form of condescension. . . .

So Bly writes his religious meditations for a public that is no longer ostensibly religious. But a more positive perspective on this "friend" would relate him to the friend addressed by George Herbert in *The Temple*. In this sense the friend is not merely a rhetorical crutch, or a way to domesticate the sublime, but the very divinity made companionable. In other words, the friend is the savior, or us, or the savior-in-us, less a social force than a private, inner healer.

> My friend, this body is made of camphor and gopherwood.
> Where it goes, we
> Follow, even into the Ark. As the light comes in sideways from
> the west over
> Damp spring buds and winter trash, the body comes out
> hesitatingly, and we are shaken, we weep, how is it that we feel
> no one has ever loved us?...

Like many American poets before him, from Whitman to Roethke, Bly believes that what Stevens called "the malady of the quotidian" must be rescued by and for the poetic consciousness. As Emerson argued, "The poet, by an ulterior intellectual perception. . . puts eyes, and a tongue into every dumb and inanimate object." So a wagonload of hay can be full of joy. . . .

Bly's poetry, in *Camphor* especially, is best understood as an attempt to get back to a pre-Orphic sense of the body. The body is sacred for Bly, because as the subject and locus of change and process, it becomes the perfect universal symbol. The body, in *Camphor*, provides the stability, while it is thought that bears the burden of "accidency and fugacity." Paradoxically, it is the very nature of the body-as-process that provides this stability. This "curiously alive and lonely body" is what loves; it "offers to carry us for nothing"; it "is made of energy compacted and whirling." And in a passage which would read more traditionally if we could reverse the poet and put "soul" where he puts "body," Bly says:

> This body longs for itself far out at sea, it floats in the black
> heavens, it is a brilliant being, locked in the prison of human
> dullness. . . .

Reprinted from The Fierce Embrace: A Study of Contemporary American Poetry *by Charles Molesworth, by permission of the University of Missouri Press. Copyright © 1979 by the Curators of the University of Missouri.*

Bly's Recent Poems

By Jonathan Blunk

Critic, translator, editor, instigator, partisan, psychologist, crank—of all the titles bestowed upon Robert Bly (whether by way of accomplishment or accusation) he is, above all else, a poet. So it's important to realize that Bly has recently published one of his finest collections of poetry. *Morning Poems* is at once a breakthrough and a distillation of his exceptional career, vital work that confronts grief and aging with wisdom and compassion.

The book's title intends a double meaning, and yet more surprising than the stunning elegies it contains is the playful humor that animates the whole collection. Bly is able to embrace both shadow and light with a sense of proportion that transcends the merely personal, as can be seen in the book's opening poem:

Early Morning in Your Room

> It's morning. The brown scoops of coffee, the wasplike
> Coffee grinder, the neighbors still asleep.
> The gray light as you pour gleaming water—
> It seems you've traveled years to get here.
>
> Finally you deserve a house. If not deserve
> It, have it; no one can get you out. Misery
> Had its way, poverty, no money at least;
> Or maybe it was confusion. But that's over.
>
> Now you have a room. Those light-hearted books:
> *The Anatomy of Melancholy*, Kafka's *Letter
> To His Father*, are all here. You can dance
> With only one leg, and see the snowflake falling
>
> With only one eye. Even the blind man
> Can see. That's what they say. If you had
> A sad childhood, so what? When Robert Burton
> Said he was melancholy, he meant he was home.

The solitary quiet that nourishes the poet includes an awareness that still sleeping neighbors are close by. Here is a solitude of maturity, even old age; the hoarse cackle heard in Samuel Beckett's work is echoed in Bly's celebration of the fruits of decay and diminishment. With this acceptance and humor comes a rich shadowing of people and things, acknowledging both human aspiration and self-deceit.

"Early Morning in Your Room" announces one of the book's recurrent scenes and themes, celebrating the solitary craftsmanship of poetry, while at the same time bringing the ear in tune to the rich patterns of sound quilted beneath Bly's thematic concerns. Notice how the dominant sound patterns divide the poem in half, with a movement away from the "er" sounds that proliferate in the first two stanzas toward the "oo" sound, as in "room," and the long "o" of "home" in the final two. In a way, this modulation toward more open and vibrant sounds underscores the poem's movement toward acceptance and affirmation. On a larger scale, the book itself is just as skillfully constructed, while retaining the spontaneous, organic feel of the individual pieces. There are dialogues with older poets and younger selves, with animals, relatives, dreams, and haystacks, all in a plain but musical language that never lapses into a didactic tone. At the heart of *Morning Poems* is a more personal and open lyrical voice.

One way to see this shift in tone—as well as the artistry worked into these poems—is to compare the sixth section of "It's as if Someone Else Is with Me" with an earlier version published in *Poetry Ireland Review* in 1994. Published separately, this poem was titled "Being Content in Your Room," and included a dedication to Wallace Stevens. The first of the poem's three stanza's has been entirely rewritten (it previously began: "How much I love giving up the wider life. . ."), and gains both greater clarity and a livelier sense of humor. The third stanza, too, is much improved:

> It's good to stay in bed a while, and hear
> The *ay* slyly hidden in sequacious,
> Scent in summer world the two *ers*,
> Listen for the *in* hidden in woodbins.
>
> Am I like the hog snuffling for truffles,
> Followed by skimpy lords in oversized furs?
> For this gaiety do I need forgiveness?
> Does the lark need forgiveness for its blue eggs?
>
> So it's a bird-like thing then, this hiding
> And warming of sounds. They are the little low
> Heavens in the nest; now my chest feathers
> Widen, now I'm an old hen, now I am satisfied.

Both humor and humility are nestled in that image of the proud poet at work on his craft; the poem with which Bly concludes *Morning Poems* makes a similar gesture. More telling, however, is a subtle change in the first line of the second stanza, lines that otherwise remain unchanged: "Is it like the hog. . ." has become "Am I like the hog. . . ," demonstrating how the poet is now more willing to fully inhabit the world of his poem.

This new confidence of voice and deepening sympathy is made possible in part by a breakthrough in form. The collection sustains a remarkable cohesiveness, relying on a loose pentameter line frequently grouped in four-line stanzas. The clipped, short lines that have often distinguished Bly's work have relaxed and lengthened, allowing the poet greater range and subtlety in "this hiding/And warming of sounds." The poem above appears so casual that one might walk right past it, even as it calls attention to its own craft. Bly avoids the showy and ponderous reliance upon sound that can be heard in lesser poems of Gerard Manley Hopkins, Dylan Thomas, or Wallace Stevens himself, where the sound of the poem is the only energy moving through it. Here the balance of sound, thought, and emotion is so assured as to disguise the artistry at work. . . .

Morning Poems reads more like a fresh beginning than a culmination, and includes some of Robert Bly's finest poetry. The collection is something of an homage to the late William Stafford, from whom Bly adopted the discipline of writing a poem every day. The unselfconscious lyrics presented here prove capable of wild leaps of imagination, and a few are quiet masterpieces. Perhaps the most generous wish anyone could bestow upon an American poet would be longevity, given the preeminent achievements of Stanley Kunitz and the exceptional late work of David Ignatow, Bly's seniors by half a generation. Here's hoping Bly's best work also lies before him.

Jonathan Blunk is a poet who lives in Peekskill, New York. This review originally appeared in The Green Mountains Review *(Vol. XI, No. 2, Fall/Winter 1998-99). Reprinted by permission of* The Green Mountains Review.

Speaking in Tongues:
The Translations of Robert Bly

By Michael Ventura

Now that our literature is rich with translations of the world's major poets, it's easy to forget that in 1970 North Americans who cared deeply for poetry had mostly never heard of the poets whom Robert Bly has since rendered so wonderfully—poets like Cesar Vallejo, Juan Ramon Jiménez, Tomas Tranströmer, Antonio Machado, Kabir, Mirabai, Rumi, and Ghalib. The little that was available before Bly, especially of the twentieth-century poets, was spotty and often clunky—or let's be kinder and say: limited. There was, for instance, only one good translator of Rainer Maria Rilke, C.F. MacIntyre, but he was best at Rilke's descriptive poetry; the spiritual marvels of *Sonnets to Orpheus* were slightly beyond his reach, and MacIntyre never translated many of Rilke's short metaphysical poems. Except for Ben Belitt's stiff but forceful rendering of Federico Garcia Lorca's *Poet in New York,* Lorca translations were rare and mostly woeful, and even Belitt had missed Lorca's fiery zest. Pablo Neruda had fared better, but rarely did his gutsy insistence on happiness, alive in even his most bitter work, make it to the North American page. Whole dimensions of Rilke, Lorca, and Neruda had to wait for Robert Bly in order to be revealed in our tongue.

Certainly by 1970 some excellent work had been done: for instance, Rex Warner's versions of George Seferis (sadly long out of print), the Rae Dalven renditions of Constantine Cavafy, and Muriel Rukeyser's presentation of Octavio Paz's *Sun Stone.* But for the most part a North American reader was unable to experience how especially twentieth-century poets of other cultures were visioning this tumultuous era. And we were desperately in need.

For by 1970 everyone knew that the United States was the dominant innovative force in modern history; the phrase "the American Century" had become, as a description, hard to deny. But that very phrase was symptomatic:

It sliced off the definition of "America" at our southern border. As Vietnam was proving so horribly, we were rich in inventiveness but impoverished in our ability to see past ourselves, to see through ourselves, and to see the validity of anything but ourselves.

Our poetry was suffering from this inflated, insulated attitude as much as our politics. It wasn't only that there were no North American poets who ranged through the underground caverns of the psyche, and linked the intimate with the historical, as vividly as Lorca, Neruda, and Vallejo; it wasn't only that a spirituality as provocative and free of boundaries and doctrine as Rilke's, Jiménez's, or Machado's was utterly absent from our poetry; and it wasn't only that the patient introspection of a Tomas Tranströmer—who conceived of contemplation as a journey, and who was too responsible to surrender to self-loathing and irony—couldn't be found in our "confessional" poets. All of that was bad enough, but it wasn't only that. It was this: that many young poets speaking and reading mainly American English, however we might yearn to go beyond William Carlos Williams' "No ideas but in things" or Robert Lowell's self-hatred or Anne Sexton's waltz with death or Allen Ginsberg's howling or Robert Creely's pinched shoes (each line a short painful step), could find no twentieth-century examples of a more expansive vision of what poetry might be.

Of the twentieth-century North American poets who had transcended the culture's more obvious limits, Hart Crane's language was too enclosed within itself to be a useful model, and the same could be said of Wallace Stevens—though both were marvelous poets. But fine poets like James Wright and David Ignatow, as well as Robert Bly, were struggling against the tide—which is why Wright and Bly often collaborated as translators, finding in translation the strength to leap past their origins and deepen their means as well as their meanings.

Then in 1971 Bly (with Wright and John Knoepfle) gave us *Neruda and Vallejo: Selected Poems*. "Compared with Vallejo," Wright wrote, "other poets seem afraid of their own voices." North American strictures weren't simply demolished by these poets; more importantly, they seemed not even to recognize our strictures, for theirs was a poetry of raw psyche that transcended the personal and ranged wherever it pleased. That book was followed in 1973 by Bly's *Lorca and Jiménez: Selected Poems*. As with the first book, Bly wisely combined a legendary name (Neruda/Lorca) with one virtually unheard of here (Vallejo/Jiménez). Bly wrote of Jiménez: "His emphasis on how the poet *lived*, rather than on rhythm and technique, is precisely why so much poetry flowed from him into the young [Spanish language] poets." Through these translations Bly was giving the same example to us. Then, using mostly translations as models, in 1975 he published *Leaping Poetry*, with a thought at its heart that for most U.S. poets was either exciting or threatening or both: "The farther a poem gets from its initial circumstance without breaking the thread, the more content it has." These forceful books, following so closely one after the other like three wild animals running suddenly past a campfire, altered the very definition of poetry for many—a coup completed with, that same year of 1975, his first translations of Tomas Tranströmer, a Swede who proved you didn't necessarily have to be Latin to leap. *The Kabir Book* followed in 1977, Tranströmer's *Truth Barriers* and the anthology *News of the Universe* (including many new translations) in 1980, *The Selected Poems of Rainer Maria Rilke* in 1981, and *Times Alone: Selected Poems of Antonio Machado* in 1983. Taken together, these nine books constitute an extraordinary and unparalleled dozen years of masterwork in translation.

Bly's translations of this period, accompanied in his many readings and essays by a constantly strong advocacy of the importance of translation, were pivotal in igniting the wave of translations that's enriched us since. Certainly no one of his generation has done as much to deepen and widen the riverbed of North American poetry. Thanks more to Bly than to anyone else, our poets have before them a universe of poetry unavailable and unimaginable thirty years ago. We're equipped now, with these models, to go into territories of the poem that stretch out limitlessly in every direction. Had he done nothing but these translations, Robert Bly would rank highly in any just evaluation of the North American pantheon.

For myself, my first book of Bly's was *Neruda and Vallejo*. I date books when I read them, and the date in my hand on the title page is 9/23/71. I was some six weeks shy of my twenty-sixth birthday, living in Brookline, Massachusetts, earning my living as a typist at the end of the trolley line in Boston—a writer who had yet to publish, working every night and far into the night on poems that I knew were terrible... but I also knew I had to write them, had to break through their inadequacies to get to whatever writing I may or may not have been born for. Why I selected this particular volume in the bookstore, I no longer remember. But I do remember that on the trolley back to my apartment I was tremendously excited by several lines of Bly's introduction, and read them over and over:

> Neruda, like a deep-sea crab, all claws and shell, is able to breathe in the heavy substances that lie beneath the daylight consciousness. He stays on the bottom for hours, and moves around calmly and without hysteria.

Getting off the trolley at my usual stop, I was too stirred up to go back to my apartment. I just walked and walked, sitting down finally on a bench in a small and lovely park where I had never been before. There I read his versions of Pablo Neruda and Cesar Vallejo for the first time. And then I wasn't reading anymore, I was remembering an old woman I'd seen years before—she was throwing handfuls of seeds all about her as a flock of pigeons flew around her and seemed

to cover and clothe her with the excited movement of their wings. On the blank back pages of that book I began writing a poem about her—with a freedom of movement within the poem that I had never attempted before the examples of Neruda and Vallejo. And then a strange thing happened: a very tall old man, well-dressed and erect, walking with a cane, passed by my bench, and he stopped, looked at me as I looked up at him, and he raised his cane and said, smiling, "Welcome to Emerson Park!"

I said, "Thank you," and we grinned at each other, and he walked on. But I felt that an emissary had been sent to me by the spirit of poetry to say, "Yes, boy, you're on the right track at last!" And he must be dead by now, long dead, but it's surprising how often I've thought of him since. Suddenly his voice and words—"Welcome to Emerson Park!"—ring in my head, and I know that some energy of that book and of my discovery within those poems had radiated to him and he'd responded with a timeless welcome. Certainly, in terms of poetry, nothing has ever been the same for me.

Michael Ventura is a poet and essayist living in Los Angeles.

Robert Bly's Leaping Influence in This World!

By James P. Lenfestey

A deep well of Minnesota's earthen energy propels Robert Bly. Consider the following list of his accomplishments, which by no means paints an exhaustive portrait.

Dozens of collections of his poetry have been published, by everyone from artist Robert Johnson's elegant Melia Press in Minneapolis to beautiful BOA Editions to trade press HarperCollins, including his 1967 National Book Award winner, *The Light Around the Body*. He has the rare distinction of having his "selected poems" brought out twice in his lifetime.

Bly authored the first important translations in English of Neruda, Vallejo, Tranströmer, Trakl, Jiménez, and many others. Most recently, he added breakthrough selections of the Middle Eastern ecstatic poets Kabir, Rumi, Mirabai, and the Indian Urdu poet Ghalib.

Bly has edited three nationally popular anthologies, all still in print: *News of the Universe*, poems of the relationship to nature; *The Rag and Bone Shop of the Heart*, subtitled "Poems for Men" but in fact universal poems of the interior landscape; and *The Soul Is Here for Its Own Joy*, poems of the spiritual landscape. What readers find so valuable about Bly's anthologies is that he makes the poetry useful. The books are organized as arguments about vital ideas or as poetry's answers to the deepest human questions and concerns.

Then there are Bly's less recognized contributions. While watching Bill Moyers' PBS series on poetry, *The Language of Life*, a few years ago (which of course included Robert as one of the featured poets), I was stunned to hear this from Coleman Barks, now famous for his highly popular English translations of the Persian poet Rumi. Barks said he had never heard of Rumi until 1976 when "Robert Bly handed me a book and said, 'These poems need to be released from their cages.'"

Flash forward to a retrospective reading of the poems of the nationally beloved poet Jane Kenyon at the Fitzgerald Theater two years ago (organized by Graywolf Press). I learned there that Robert had been a friend of Jane's for decades, and it was he who gave her the poems of Anna Akhmatova to translate, work which helped launch her career.

These are only two of many examples of Bly's impact on revered poets. In fact, Bly is regularly asked to participate in poetry conferences around the world—Sweden, Norway, Germany, North Africa, the Canary Islands, and London are the places I know about. At the invitation of internationally acclaimed poet Andrei Voznesensky, he recently participated in a writer's conference in Moscow.

For Robert Bly and his audience, poetry is the food of human life, slaking our daily hunger for connection to the world, our hearts, our souls. To attend a Bly reading, or to read an essay or article by him, is to be amazed. He quotes like scripture the lines and poems of dozens of world poets from his encyclopedic memory as if the words were those of prophets and philosophers.

Personal case in point. This year I chaired a nonprofit organization based in Los Angeles, the Environmental Media Association, the interface between Hollywood and national environmental groups. At our annual awards ceremony in January, I recited from the podium a poem by turn-of-the-century Spanish poet Antonio Machado, translated, of course, by Robert Bly.

> The wind, one brilliant day, called
> to my soul with the odor of jasmine.
>
> "In return for the odor of my jasmine,
> I'd like all the odor of your roses."
>
> "I have no roses; all the flowers
> in my garden are dead."
>
> "Well then, I'll take the withered petals
> and the yellow leaves and the waters of the fountain."
>
> The wind left. And I wept. And I said to myself:
> "What have you done with the garden that was entrusted to you?"

How had I come to memorize this poem? Because I heard it recited at small gatherings around winter campfires, at large readings, at discussions of poetry at The Loft. A neighborhood friend quoted it by heart to me one morning over coffee. Now I carry it within me. Because of Robert's translation, this poem moves through our culture like life-giving water.

Consider another story from my own experience. As a graduate student at the University of Wisconsin in 1967-69, I read copies of Bly's magazines from Madison, Minnesota, *The Fifties* and *The Sixties*. In the early '70s, I sent some of my poems to *The Seventies*. Months later I was stunned to receive a handwritten reply from Bly himself, offering valuable particular comments on my poems, and this general observation: "But overall they are not really poems."

I was angry at him for a decade! How dare he judge what was and was not a poem! Years later I came across his book of essays, *Leaping Poetry*. It defines what he believes a true poem must do—leap from the conscious, particular world to the unconscious, universal one, like a person daring to reach blindly through a wall with one arm. And I understood finally what he had meant ten years before. I realized too that he was right.

In a 1970 edition of the *Tennessee Poetry Journal*, Bly, in colloquy with William Stafford and other national poets on the topic of small literary magazines, told how he came to write such notes, given that magazines ordinarily respond with preprinted rejections. He believed a generalized note did the poet no good. It was much better to say the poems were terrible than to blandly imply "no room." In that way he challenged thousands of poets to better work. He still does.

Although Bly is one of America's best-known poets, his local impact in Minnesota has been profound in multiple ways. His was the first benefit reading ever given at The Loft, then a single room over a small bookstore, now the largest literary center in the nation. I remember driving in from Wisconsin in the late '60s to attend a poetry reading Bly organized against the war in Vietnam. The large hall at the University of Minnesota was jammed. I still have his poem he read that day, "The Teeth Mother Naked at Last," published by City Lights Books of San Francisco.

Robert Bly's seemingly quixotic decision to return to an old farmhouse in Madison, Minnesota, to cultivate the ground of world poetry has helped remake the literary landscape. Witness the citizens of Madison, who, at their own expense, rehabilitated Bly's old writing studio and turned it into a treasured town landmark!

Poet Thomas R. Smith said at the dedication of the restored Robert Bly Writing Studio last year, "Perhaps Robert's greatest gift to Madison is that through his poems he has given Madison to the world." Bly also gave Midwestern writers the confidence to find the universal in the silent spaces of their snowy fields, in the vast length of a curled oak leaf by a lake.

Robert Bly is in his seventies now, still vigorous, still traveling around the world on an exhausting schedule. And still coming home to Minnesota. Not New York. Not San Francisco. Not Paris. But Minnesota, helping make this state like few others the center of a vibrant, living literary culture where poetry is used, like the plows in our fields, to help us grow.

James P. Lenfestey is a poet and writer living in the Twin Cities. He is a former teacher, marketing communications consultant, and editorial writer for the Minneapolis Star Tribune.

Praising the Soul in Women and Men: Robert Bly and the Men's Movement

BY THOMAS R. SMITH

Nineteen-ninety, the watershed year for the men's movement in the U.S., was also, not coincidentally, the year that rocketed Robert Bly, along with his best-selling book *Iron John*, to international media visibility.

Interviewing Bly for *New Age Journal*, Jeff Wagenheim asked a question apparently puzzling many: Why a *poet* leading this men's movement, and not a politician, say, or a sports hero?

Characteristically deflecting emphasis from himself, Bly replied, "One reason poetry is at the center is because the language that men use to communicate with each other has gotten very damaged." Bly's answer, though utterly consistent with his fifty-plus-year career as a defender of the beauty, depth, and nourishing power of language, begs the question, Why *this* poet?

In fact, Bly's intellectual engagement with gender matters reaches back at least to his 1973 essay, "I Came Out of the Mother Naked." Building on Jung's theory of the coexistence of both masculine and feminine traits in the psyche, Bly's essay stands as a touchstone for much of his subsequent thought on the sexes. He wrote: "All my clumsy prose amounts to is praise of the feminine soul, whether that soul appears in men or women." He added, tellingly, "The masculine soul . . . also needs praise, but I am not doing that here."

Although the '70s for Bly were very much a time of "praising the feminine soul," his attention would soon swing toward the masculine in the '80s. Bly had taught the spiritual and cultural values of matriarchy at his annual Conference on the Great Mother since 1975, but in 1981, by request, he taught a group of men for the first time at the Lama Commune in Taos, New Mexico.

Perhaps this new men's work became Bly's way of dealing with midlife crisis, or facing more directly the emotional legacy of a kind and upstanding but alcoholic father. He told Clarissa Pinkola Estés in 1991 that he'd at first thought, "My male side was developed, and my feminine side was not developed. . . . [But] what I developed is the *shallow* form of the masculine, and what I need now is to develop the *deeper* form of the masculine, of which feeling is a part."

That quest, of course, led directly to *Iron John*, Bly's often brilliant exploration of the Grimm Brothers' tale in which a boy discovers, in the person of a "wild man" covered with rust-colored hair at the bottom of a pond, a powerful teacher. Emphasizing the tempering of a man's psyche through grief work, *Iron John* proposed an expressive alternative to the stoicism of traditional masculinity. Beneath the colorful mix of poetry, mythology, psychology, and social commentary lay a brooding conviction that the emotional isolation and violence of American men masks a hunger for fathering and male mentoring, diminished in a time of multiplying divorce rates and single-parent households.

In the year that *Iron John* unbudgingly roosted atop bestseller lists, small "mythopoetic" men's groups sprang up by the hundreds nationwide. *Newsweek*'s cover for June 24, 1991, displayed a grinning, bare-chested CEO holding a toddler in one arm and a conga drum in the other. Probably no one was more surprised than its author when the book Bly described as simply "an amplification of a fairy story" became a de facto bible for what appeared to be a genuine mass movement. In *Esquire* (October 1991), Bly maintained caution: "A movement implies a doctrine. I just say something is stirring."

Something else that stirred, perhaps inevitably, was hostility from women and men who feared that Bly's activity on behalf of men must also be *against* women, a kind of reasoning Bly has often skewered as "oppositional thinking." In an inflammatory and ill-conceived tirade in the March/April 1992 *Ms.*, Sharon Doubiago even accused Bly of supporting the Persian Gulf War, choosing to ignore his courageous and well-documented record as a peace activist.

Despite such attacks, Bly continued to fill lecture halls and retreat centers, appearing often with the psychologist James Hillman and the storyteller Michael Meade into the mid-'90s. To further stress the importance of poetry as an essential inner resource for men, the three co-edited the massive poetry anthology *The Rag and Bone Shop of the Heart*, arguably the best of its decade.

Since that time, Bly's men's conferences, though fewer and no longer deemed newsworthy by the media, have taken on a more activist tone, with a shift of focus from personal or internal to societal concerns. Part of Bly's genius lies in his ability to open these conferences to such remarkable teachers as the Mayan artist and shaman Martín Prechtel and the innovative prison reformer Bob Roberts. Bly has also introduced to the mostly white middle-class participants outstanding teachers of color such as poet Haki Madhubuti, healer Malidoma Somé, and percussionist Miguel Rivera.

Ten years down the road, the issues that ignited Bly's burst of high visibility in the early '90s have not gone away. In fact, they have intensified. Incidents such as the tragic shootings in Littleton chillingly corroborate Bly's observation that the souls of boys, as well as girls, are under siege in consumer society. Many women seem to agree now with Bly's contention that socializing younger men is primarily the job of older men, a source of bitter gender controversy in the early '90s.

Meanwhile, Bly continues writing poems and essays praising the soul in men and women, some of which revisit his abiding interest in the ancient matriarchal civilizations. His 1998 collaboration with Marion Woodman, *The Maiden King*, examines a Russian story about a young man's initiation not into the masculine but the mysteries of the feminine, "which through long years of patriarchal culture we have forgotten." In his 1973 essay, Bly wrote: "[In the matriarchies] each man was once with the Mother—having gone out into masculine consciousness, a man's job is to return." Indeed, that is the arc that his life and work appear to be following.

While the ideas and images of the movement for which Bly was chosen unlikely spokesman have been superficially absorbed by mainstream society, meaningful change has lagged behind. In a *Paris Review* interview, Bly quotes a recent Dewar's ad ("You don't need to beat a drum or hug a tree to be a man") and remarks: "The corporate world dares to say to young men, knowing how much young men want to be men, that the only requirement for manhood is to become an alcoholic. That's disgusting. It's a tiny indication of the ammunition aimed at men who try to learn to talk or to feel."

This spring, when asked by the Minneapolis *Star Tribune* which activities he would propose for a national day for boys equivalent to Take Our Daughters to Work day, Bly suggested that fathers take their sons to the library and show them the books they love. Noting that women have often been excluded from the work world, Bly said, "I think it's just as likely now that men will be shut out of the inward world, the literature world." That is at the heart of what Robert Bly has been saying these past decades, to the many or the few.

Thomas R. Smith is a poet and essayist living in River Falls, Wisconsin.

Poems

By Robert Bly

The Night Abraham Called to the Stars

Do you remember the night Abraham first saw
The stars? He cried to Saturn: "You are my Lord!"
How happy he was! When he saw the Dawn Star,

He cried, "You are my Lord!" How destroyed he was
When he watched them set. Friends, he is like us:
We take as our Lord the stars that go down.

We are faithful companions to the unfaithful stars.
We are diggers, like badgers; we love to feel
The dirt flying out from behind our back claws.

And no one can convince us that mud is not
Beautiful. It is our badger soul that thinks so.
We are ready to spend the rest of our life

Walking with muddy shoes in the wet fields.
We resemble exiles in the kingdom of the serpent.
We stand in the onion fields looking up at the night.

My heart is a calm potato by day, and a weeping
Abandoned woman by night. Friend, tell me what to do,
Since I am a man in love with the setting stars.

Thinking of *Gitanjali*

A man is walking along thinking of *Gitanjali*,
And a mink leaps out from under a log. I don't know
Why it is I want you to sit on my lap,
Or why it is our children speak to us lovingly.

Answering that is like plotting one's
Political life by listening to Schubert, or letting
The length of your poem be decided by how
Many times the goldfish turns in his bowl.

I do remember that boy in the third grade
Who said, "We're friends, but let's fight!"
So affection intricately inserts itself.
The story makes sense, I guess, like everything

Else that happened when you were
On your way to school. And those gestures
Of love our mother gave us we saved
Somewhere, as Tagore did, until they

Became evidence of the love of God.

"Thinking of Gitanjali" *appeared in* Eating the Honey of Words: New and Selected Poems
*(HarperCollins Publishers, New York, 1999). Copyright © 1999 by Robert Bly. Reprinted by permission
of HarperCollins Publishers Inc.*

Night

I

If I think of a horse wandering about sleeplessly
All night on this short grass covered with moonlight,
I feel a joy, as if I had thought
Of a pirate ship ploughing through dark flowers.

II

The box elders around us are full of joy,
Obeying what is beneath them.
The lilacs are sleeping, and the plants are sleeping,
Even the wood made into a casket is asleep.

III

The butterfly is carrying loam on his wings;
The toad is bearing tiny bits of granite in his skin;
The leaves at the crown of the tree are asleep
Like the dark bits of earth at its root.

IV

Alive, we are like a sleek black water beetle,
Skating across still water in any direction
We choose, and soon to be swallowed
Suddenly from beneath.

Reprinted from Silence in the Snowy Fields *(Wesleyan University Press, Middletown, CT, 1962).*
Copyright © 1962 Robert Bly. Reprinted with his permission.

From "Captain Bly"

By Ted Solotaroff

Like most literary careers that last, Robert Bly's has been formed from the ongoing play of oppositions, but his have been particularly intense: Lutheran and pagan, rural and international, reclusive and engaged, austere and grandiose. These contending traits and inclinations have generated Bly's high energy and also created a certain rhythm to his career that makes his present celebrity and function almost predictable. . . .

Much of Bly's soul has been forged and refined by his relationship with the Wild Man, the tutelary figure in *Iron John*, the fairy tale that he unpacks and embroiders to tell the reader how boys psychically become men and men remain psychically boys.

Bly grew up, as he says, a "Lutheran boy-god" in Minnesota, being his mother's favorite. . . . Bly's brother appears to have been his father's son, the one who took up the family occupation of farming, the hairy Esau to his tent-dwelling Jacob. His father was strong, kindly, intensely moral, and alcoholic, creating a particularly poignant remoteness that broods over *Iron John*, as it does in some of Bly's later poetry: "the man in the black coat" who appears only to turn away again and whose haunting absence, along with his mother's haunting presence, has created Bly's lifelong project and process of fathering one's soul. . . .

Bly doesn't talk about his Harvard experience in *Iron John*—he seldom has in a career otherwise rich in self-revelation—but it was a determinate stage in which this wounded boy-god and naive "ascender" was both endowed and banished, a literary version of the prince of his fairy tale. Here he is as an editor of the *Harvard Advocate*, reviewing a collection of British poetry edited by Kenneth Rexroth. One sentence tells the tale: "Perhaps it is unfortunate that Rexroth should have been let loose on the Romantics; there is, I think, a difference between the desire to express personal emotion by increased direct reference to the world of nature, and the desire to overthrow all external discipline of morals of government."

This is, of course, the T. S. Eliot act that many young literary men in the postwar era imitated to put themselves on what they took to be the cutting edge of modernism. In Bly's case, it suggests that he was turning over in his sleep from the Lutheran law to the Anglican one. The literary air at the time was thick with conservative authority and decorum. It had an archbishop, Eliot; a set of bishops, the New Critics; a martyr, Pound; and lots of acolytes, who were becoming half-paralyzed by the dogma that poetry was a hieratic vocation, that the imagination lived, worked, and had its being within The Tradition. As Eliot had laid it down, The Tradition was mostly Dante and the metaphysical poets, who were high Anglicans like himself. The dogma came equipped with Eliot's emphasis on the impersonal, objective image and with a set of literary heresies and fallacies that were meant to nip any revival of Romanticism in the bud. . . .

The one poem that Bly published from this period, "Where We Must Look for Help," is based on the three birds that were sent forth from Noah's ark into the flooded world: The glamorous peaceful dove and the graceful swallows find no land, only the crow does:

> The crow, the crow, the spider-colored crow,
> The crow shall find new mud to walk upon.

As Bly was to tell Deborah Baker, who has written an excellent biographical essay about him ("Making a Farm: A Literary Biography," *Poetry East*, 4 and 5, Spring/Summer 1981, pp. 145-186), "It was the first time I ran into the idea of the dark side of the personality being the fruitful one." After a year at the Iowa Writers' Workshop, Bly went to live on a farm his father had bought for him, and a year later, while visiting relatives in Norway, he discovered his new mud lying adjacent to his inner tradition. . . .

In "Looking for Dragon Smoke," Bly hooked together a countertradition to the Christian/rational/industrial one, providing a kind of culture of the Wild Man. It begins with *Gilgamesh*, in which the "psychic forces" of an early civilized society created the hairy, primitive Enkidu as the adversary and eventual companion of the golden Gilgamesh (a harbinger of *Iron John*). After *Beowulf* (Bly's Nordic touchstone), the "dragon smoke" of inspired association with primal memories is not much in evidence until Blake arrives to give the lie to the Enlightenment, as do the associative freedom and "pagan and heretical elements" in his German contemporaries Novalis, Goethe, and Hölderlin. With Freud and Jung the unconscious is back in business again, and the romantic/symbolist/surrealist wing of modernism provides Bly with a whole range of leaping, dragon-smoke poets from Scandinavia south to Spain and across to Latin America to translate, publish, and emulate. . . .

He supported himself by his public appearances; otherwise he remained on his farm, tending to his chores as an editor, publisher, critic, and poet and using his solitude to nourish "the parts that grow when we are far from the centers of ambition." Through the writings of Jung, Joseph Campbell, James Hillman, and other psychic/cultural explorers, he developed his encyclopedic command of the great heuristic myths, legends, and folklore that understand us, concentrating on those that involve the female side. He gave lectures on Freud and Jung, as well as on *Grimm's Fairy Tales*, in the church basement in Madison, his trial by fire in making the esoteric vivid and meaningful to the public. He turned from America's shadow to his own, producing eleven collections of poems, most of them inward, associative, naked—Bly fully joining the tradition he had been staking out. . . .

The souled fierceness that he prescribes for staking out and protecting the borders of male identity has provided much of the motive energy for his career as a literary radical. By the same token, his devotion to asserting and cultivating the primalness and primacy of the imagination in a highly domesticated and institutionalized literary culture has led him to view the condition of men in similar terms and to apply the learning he has acquired in the archaeology and anthropology of the imagination to remedy it. This authority is finally what makes *Iron John* a serious, groundbreaking book.

Ted Solotaroff was for thirty years the literary editor and is now a contributing editor of The Nation. *He was also a founding editor of the* New American Review. *The full article from which this is excerpted originally appeared in* The Nation *(Vol. 253, No. 7, Sept. 9, 1991). Reprinted by permission of* The Nation.

Among Friends

REMINISCENCES ABOUT ROBERT BLY

Marion Woodman
Jungian psychologist and author
London, Ontario

With his say-it-like-it-is, gusty, and sensitive voice, he constellates the king, the warrior, the child, the trickster. That is why I feel so challenged working with him. I never know what will happen next. We move from swan shirts to mouse steak to leaping firebirds with alarming ease. We have even been known to disappear. We were once sitting on a raised platform on a stage—with perhaps a little too much king and queen in the air. Suddenly, I realized his chair was moving back as if two mighty hands were pulling from behind. I was so curious about his chair that I didn't realize my own had begun to move. The next thing I knew we were both flat on our backs behind the platform, buried under wires and microphones with four little stockinged feet waving in the air. That changed the archetypes at that conference!

Nils Peterson
Poet
Campbell, California

What Robert catches are those moments when the vertical and the "prosaically horizontal life" twist against each other. As we read them in his poetry, we feel in our bodies the reality of that torsion. Our heads nod yes. Something in our throats makes a little sound telling us we are in the presence of a true thing, and something turns us back into the process of thinking about and living our own story. That is one of the gifts of Robert's poetry and of Robert himself.

Marv Davidov
Honeywell Project leader and activist
Minneapolis, Minnesota

Later one hundred of us were tried in a mass trial, with fourteen people representing the whole group. Robert testified before the jury, quoting Thoreau. In his closing statement he said to the jury, "The prosecutor would have tried to get Jesus for trespass." He said, "The prosecutor has erected a wall. There is a little passage at the bottom of this wall. You can crawl through like mice to the other side, or you can struggle through and stand up like human beings." They crawled through like mice and convicted us, and the judge sent one hundred of us to the workhouse for a few days.

Donald Hall
Poet
Danbury, New Hampshire

In February of 1948 I went out for the *Harvard Advocate* and met the austere figure of Robert Bly. He was twenty-one; I was nineteen. He was skinny, never smiled, and wore three-piece suits with narrow striped ties; he was very very intelligent. If we had not met, how would our lives have differed? My life would have been poorer, thinner, less energetic; there would have been less excitement and less confrontation. For more than forty years we have talked about poetry, politics, and the spirit; we have argued, we have exalted and blasted each other. We perform a friendship of opposites, Heraclitean enantiodromia, as we square off at every crossroads: Plato and Aristotle, Jung and Freud, whirlpool and rock, Don Quixote and Sancho Panza. If neither of us has published anything without showing it to the other, each of us has disobediently published work that the other loathed. Contradiction or conflict is probably more important to friendship than coherence; certainly it creates more. I owe him so much, I cannot imagine my life without him.

Gioia Timpanelli
Storyteller and author
Woodstock, New York

While Robert is a generous friend, not stingy or mean-spirited, I wouldn't want to give the impression he's flawless. But then you don't have to know Robert very well to know his willingness to show his "shadow side." John Keats, in a letter to his brother and sister-in-law (April 21, 1819), wrote, "The common cognomen of this world among the misguided and superstitious is 'a vale of tears.' . . . Call the world if you please 'The vale of Soul-making.' . . . Then you will find out the use of the world." I would say that Robert's great heart and desire for knowledge and poetry and intuition and thinking and writing and shadow sides are all part of this great soul-making in him.

Bill Holm
Poet and essayist
Minneota, Minnesota

He [Robert] made us feel, in "The Teeth Mother Naked at Last," our unescapable connection as humans and as citizens to the psychic and political life of our community, our country. He did this like no one since Whitman. Our wars take place not only in Vietnam, or Panama, or Iraq, but inside us. Every complaint the academics make of "The Teeth Mother" is true; it is excessive, rhetorical, preachy. But watch an audience of Americans listen to it, read by Robert or by any passionate voice that can do it justice. They are bolted, fixed, trapped by it. They weep. Best of all, they think, for years afterwards.

Jane Kenyon
Poet
(1947-1995)

I t was Robert who urged me to translate Anna Akhmatova's poems, and who, along with Louis Simpson, appealed to Vera Dunham to work with me. Robert had come to visit us for a few days in New Hampshire. He asked what I was working on, read it thoughtfully. "It's time for you to choose a poet dead or alive and work with that poet as a master," he said. That way of reading had never occurred to me. "I cannot choose a man for a master," I said. "Then read Akhmatova," said Robert. . . .

For five years I sat at Akhmatova's feet. What Robert told me was true: Whatever work you put into translation comes back to you like the twelve baskets of bread and fish left after the feeding of the five thousand. It's to Robert that I owe the book, and to him the deep changes that occurred in my own poems as a result of that work.

Robert Moore
Jungian psychologist and author
Chicago, Illinois

E rikson believed that the way great cultural innovators act upon their age is that their own personal issues and problems coincide with some of the central problems of their age. In seeking to deal with their own problems, great men—cultural innovators—help their culture address these issues on a wide scale. It is my belief that Robert Bly's contribution to our culture and our time may— when evaluated by historians of the future—prove to have been an example of the dynamic that Erikson has noted. Robert is, I believe, a great poet. But his true greatness lies in the way in which he has, in struggling with his own masculine wounds, enabled an entire generation of men around the world to begin asking some of the most significant questions of our time.

Barbara McClintock
Executive Director
Joseph Campbell Archives and Library
Pacifica Graduate Institute
Santa Barbara, California

D uring the fifteen years that I have worked with Robert at large public events, I have been touched many times by this man's gentle gift of compassion, spontaneously evoked when he encounters a fellow sufferer. However frenzied the moment, he downshifts in the presence of someone who is hurt or ashamed or darkly aggrieved. I am reminded of his own statement concerning his artistic intention: to merge in a poem his personal consciousness with a second consciousness, outside of himself, that "has a melancholy tone, the tear inside the stone . . . an energy circling downward, felt often in autumn, or moving slowly around apple trees or stars." It occurs to me that this "artistic intention" reflects, not surprisingly, the intention of Robert's heart—to merge with the tear in the stone or in the eye.

A Poet's Life

1926
Born December 23 in Madison, Minnesota.

1944
Serves in the U.S. Navy for two years.

1946-47
Transfers from St. Olaf College to Harvard, where he joins Archibald MacLeish's writing class, along with Adrienne Rich, Donald Hall, John Ashbery, Kenneth Koch, and others.

1951-53
Lives a "garret life" working at part-time jobs in New York City.

1954
Spends a year in the Writers' Workshop in Iowa City, and teaches at the University of Iowa.

1955
Marries Carolyn McLean and settles on a farm near Madison, where they will raise four children, Mary, Bridget, Noah, and Micah.

1956-57
Awarded Fulbright Fellowship to Norway, where he discovers the work of South American and Spanish poets and decides to introduce them in English translation through a new literary magazine.

As a child in Madison, Minnesota

At Harvard

With daughters Bridget and Mary

Bly's old study (once a chicken house)

1958

Publishes first issue of *The Fifties* with William Duffy. The inside cover says, "All the poetry published in the U.S. today is too old-fashioned."

1962

Publishes first volume of poems, *Silence in the Snowy Fields.*

1963

Awarded a Guggenheim Fellowship and an Amy Lowell Traveling Fellowship.

1966

Organizes, with David Ray, a national group called American Writers Against the Vietnam War.

1968

Receives the National Book Award for *The Light Around the Body*. At the award ceremony he counsels refusal to serve in the military and turns the award money over to the antiwar movement.

With William Duffy tearing up *The Saturday Review of Literature*

1970

Lives in Point Reyes, California for a year.

1979

Carolyn and Robert Bly divorce.

1980

Marries Ruth Ray and moves to the Moose Lake area, where the younger children and Ruth's children, Sam and Wesley, live.

Cover of the first issue of *The Fifties*

1982

Teaches a group of men for the first time at Lama Commune in Taos, New Mexico, and in the next years leads, with Michael Meade, James Hillman, and

A reading with David Whetstone (sitar) and Marcus Wise (tablas), Toronto, 1991

With grandson Luca

During the Vietnam era

Robert Moore, workshops and conferences for men, teaching material that will eventually become *Iron John*.

1987

Inducted into the American Academy of Arts and Letters.

1989

A Bill Moyers documentary on Bly, *A Gathering of Men*, brings the men's work Bly has been involved with for five years to the public eye. A companion documentary, *On Being a Man*, is produced by KTCA-TV.

1990-91

Iron John rises to top of the *New York Times* bestseller list. Bly becomes a vocal critic of the Gulf War.

1992

Marion Woodman and Robert Bly do a six-hour documentary on the Russian story "The Maiden King." Their book is published in 1998.

1994

First grandchild, Luca, is born. Three others, Nora, Anna, and Zoe, follow.

1990-2000

Continues to lead, with Gioia Timpanelli, Martín Prechtel, Ruth Bly, John Lee, and others, the Conference on the Great Mother and the New Father, centering on poetry and ritual. Continues to hold men's conferences as well. Publishes *Morning Poems* (1997) and *Eating the Honey of Words: New and Selected Poems* (1999).

Publications by Robert Bly

POETRY

Silence in the Snowy Fields, 1962

The Light Around the Body, 1967

Sleepers Joining Hands, 1973

Jumping Out of Bed, 1973

This Tree Will Be Here for a Thousand Years, 1979

The Man in the Black Coat Turns, 1981

Loving a Woman in Two Worlds, 1985

Selected Poems, 1986

Meditations on the Insatiable Soul, 1994

Morning Poems, 1997

Eating the Honey of Words: New and Selected Poems, 1999

PROSE POEMS

The Morning Glory, 1975

This Body Is Made of Camphor and Gopherwood, 1977

What Have I Ever Lost by Dying?, 1992

PROSE

Talking All Morning (Interviews), 1980

The Eight Stages of Translation, 1983

A Little Book on the Human Shadow (with William Booth), 1986

American Poetry: Wildness and Domesticity, 1990

Iron John: A Book About Men, 1990

Remembering James Wright, 1991

The Sibling Society, 1996

The Maiden King: The Reunion of Masculine and Feminine (with Marion Woodman), 1998

TRANSLATIONS

The Story of Gosta Berling
by Selma Lagerlof, 1961

Twenty Poems of Georg Trakl
(with James Wright), 1961

Hunger by Knut Hamsun, 1967

Neruda and Vallejo: Selected Poems
(with James Wright and
John Knoepfle), 1971

Lorca and Jiménez: Selected Poems, 1973

Friends, You Drank Some Darkness:
Three Swedish Poets, Martinson,
Ekelof, and Tranströmer, 1975

The Kabir Book: 44 of the Ecstatic Poems
of Kabir, 1977

Twenty Poems of Rolf Jacobsen, 1977

Twenty Poems of Vincente Aleixandre
(with Lewis Hyde), 1977

Truth Barriers (Tomas Tranströmer),
1980

Selected Poems of Rainer Maria Rilke,
1981

Times Alone: Selected Poems
of Antonio Machado, 1983

When Grapes Turn to Wine (Rumi),
1983

Trusting Your Life to Water
and Eternity: Twenty Poems of
Olav H. Hauge, 1987

Ten Poems of Francis Ponge Translated
by Robert Bly and Two Poems
of Robert Bly Inspired by the Poems
of Francis Ponge, 1990

The Lightning Should Have Fallen on
Ghalib (with Sunil Dutta), 1999

EDITOR

A Poetry Reading Against the Vietnam
War (with David Ray), 1966

The Sea and the Honeycomb: 80 Tiny
Poems, 1966

Forty Poems Touching on Recent
American History, 1966

Leaping Poetry, 1975

News of the Universe: Poems of Twofold
Consciousness, 1980

The Winged Life: Selected Poems and
Prose of Thoreau, 1986

The Rag and Bone Shop of the Heart
(with James Hillman and Michael
Meade), 1992

The Darkness Around Us Is Deep:
Selected Poems of William Stafford,
1993

The Soul Is Here for Its Own Joy: Sacred
Poems from Many Cultures, 1995

The Best American Poetry, 1999

About the Award

Minnesota is often cited as a special place to live because its citizens have access to such a wealth of cultural activities. Theaters, museums and galleries, dance programs, performances, music, and films enliven our storefronts and street corners, our stages and concert halls. But we often forget who set all this activity in motion.

The Distinguished Artist Award, now in its third year, recognizes those who, individually and collectively, laid the foundation for what we enjoy today. Although they had opportunities to pursue their work elsewhere, they chose to stay, and by staying made a difference. These artists have founded and/or strengthened Minnesota's vibrant arts organizations, mentored and inspired younger artists, and attracted audiences and patrons who enable art to thrive. Most of all, they are working artists who have made the most of their formidable talents.

Many of these artists have received national or international honors. But, despite the state's rich cultural history, there was no appropriate tribute for them at home. The Distinguished Artist Award—a Minnesota award for Minnesota artists—seeks to fill that gap.

One artist each year receives the award, which includes a $40,000 stipend. Anyone is welcome to nominate an artist. Nominations received by March 31 will be considered the same year. A panel of people appointed on the basis of their knowledge of Minnesota's cultural history reviews the nominations, may suggest others, and selects the distinguished artist.

This year's panelists considered more than one hundred artists from all over the state before reaching a unanimous decision. Our thanks to Linda Hoeschler, executive director of the American Composers Forum, St. Paul; Linda Myers, executive director of The Loft Literary Center, Minneapolis; Thomas O'Sullivan, past curator at the Minnesota Historical Society, St. Paul; and the late Mike Steele, former staff writer for the Minneapolis *Star Tribune,* who passed away in May 2000. Mike was a valued member of the selection panel since the award's inception, and will be missed. The panel members have set a high standard that makes this award all the more meaningful in documenting Minnesota's cultural history.

Neal Cuthbert
Program Director, Arts
The McKnight Foundation

McKnight Distinguished Artists

Robert Bly   2000

Warren MacKenzie   1999

Dominick Argento   1998

The McKnight Foundation
600 TCF Tower
121 South Eighth Street
Minneapolis, MN 55402
612-333-4220
www.mcknight.org

Special thanks to Ally Press
for permission to reprint excerpts
from *Walking Swiftly: Writings
in Honor of Robert Bly*, and to
Thomas Smith for his generous
assistance.

Design
    Barbara Koster
Photography
    Mark Luinenburg
Editing
    Gayle Thorsen
Printing
    Diversified Graphics Incorporated
    on Mohawk Options made with
    20% postconsumer fiber

The Mill, the Stone, and the Water

All our desire is a grain of wheat.
Our whole personality is the milling-building.
But this mill grinds without knowing about it.

The mill stone is your heavy body.
What makes the stone turn is your thought-river.
The stone says: I don't know why we do all this, but the river has knowledge!

If you ask the river, it says,
I don't know why I flow.
All I know is that a human opened the gate!

And if you ask the person, he says:
All I know, oh gobbler of bread, is that if this stone
Stops going around, there'll be no bread for your bread-soup!

All this grinding goes on, and no one has any knowledge!
So just be quiet, and one day turn
To God, and say: "What is this about bread-making?"

Rumi (translation, Robert Bly)

Reprinted from The Soul Is Here for Its Own Joy: Sacred Poems from Many Cultures *(ed. Robert Bly, Ecco Press, Hopewell, NJ, 1995). Copyright ©1995 Robert Bly. Reprinted with his permission.*